THE APACHES

BY ALISON BEHNKE

CONSULTANT: KARL A. HOERIG, PH.D., MUSEUM DIRECTOR,
NOHWIKÉ BAGOWA THE WHITE MOUNTAIN APACHE
CULTURAL CENTER AND MUSEUM

LERNER PUBLICATIONS COMPANY
MINNEAPOLIS

ABOUT THE COVER IMAGE: This Apache basket is made of plant fibers. In the past, the Apaches made baskets like this one to gather corn and other food. Today they are used in ceremonies.

PHOTO ACKNOWLEDGMENTS:
The images in this book are used with the permission of: Courtesy of the Division of Anthropology, American Museum of Natural History, 50/8702, pp. 1 (background), 3 (background), 4 (background), 18 (background), 28 (background), 40 (background); Library of Congress, pp. 5 (LC-USZ62-106984), 8 (LC-USZ62-104919), 11 (LC-USZ62-46945), 14 (LC-USZ62-104713), 15 (LC-USZ62-112830), 19 (LC-USZ62-111349), 20 (LC-DIG-stereo-1s00347), 21 (LC-USZ62-37993), 22 (LC-USZC4-8856), 26 (HABS ARIZ,12-TUBA.V,1-2), 30 (LC-USZC4-9950), 36 (LC-USZ62-101172), 37 (LC-USZC4-8838), 38 (LC-USZC2-6298), 39 (LC-USZ6-1750), 41 (LC-USZ62-95795); © Laura Westlund/IPS, p. 6; © Brown Brothers, p. 7; © North Wind Picture Archives, pp. 9, 12, 13, 17, 24, 31, 32, 34; National Archives, p. 10 (NWDNS-77-WF-59); Courtesy of the Arizona Historical Society/Tucson, 30392, p. 16; © Marilyn "Angel" Wynn/Nativestock.com, p. 25; © Bettmann/CORBIS, p. 27; © SuperStock, Inc./SuperStock, pp. 29, 35; Cochise by William S. Sutton, 1872 © Charles Parker, p. 33; © Peter Turnley/CORBIS, p. 42; © Ernst Haas/Hulton Archive/Getty Images, p. 43; © Raymond Bial, p. 44; © Inn of the Mountain Gods Resort & Casino, p. 45; © AP/Wide World Photos, p. 47; Photo by Lee Marmon, Courtesy of the Allan Houser Foundation Archives, p. 48; © Anders Ryman/CORBIS, p. 49; © Catherine Karnow/CORBIS, p. 50.

Front Cover: Courtesy of the Division of Anthropology, American Museum of Natural History, 50/8677

Lerner Publications Company
A division of Lerner Publishing Group
241 First Avenue North
Minneapolis, MN 55401 U.S.A.

Website address: www.lernerbooks.com

Library of Congress Cataloging-in-Publication Data

Behnke, Alison.
    The Apaches / by Alison Behnke.
      p. cm. — (Native American histories)
    Includes bibliographical references and index.
    ISBN-13: 978-0-8225-5915-3 (lib. bdg : alk. paper)
    ISBN-10: 0-8225-5915-3 (lib. bdg : alk. paper)
    1. Apache Indians—History—Juvenile literature. 2. Apache Indians—Social life and customs—Juvenile literature. I. Title. II. Series.
    E99.A6S75 2007
    979.004'9725—dc22   2005032219

Manufactured in the United States of America
1 2 3 4 5 6 – DP – 12 11 10 09 08 07

CONTENTS

CHAPTER 1

ANCIENT WAYS

THE APACHE PEOPLE HAVE LIVED IN NORTH AMERICA FOR HUNDREDS OF YEARS. They are often known as Native Americans or American Indians. But the Apaches call themselves the Ndee. This name is also sometimes spelled Inde, Nide, or Tinde. It means "the People." Outsiders gave the People the name Apache.

The Apaches are made up of many different but related groups. They all share certain traditions and a language. But they also have their own established ways. The main Apache groups are the Mescalero, Jicarilla, Chiricahua, Lipan, Kiowa-Apache, and Western Apaches.

Chief Hunting Horse *(center)* and his daughters posed for this picture in 1908. They are Kiowa-Apache. The Kiowa-Apache people are one of six main Apache groups.

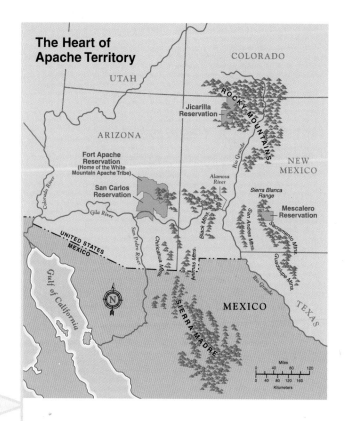

The Heart of Apache Territory

This map shows the central part of the Apaches' traditional homeland.

HOUSE AND HOME

The historic Apache homeland stretched from modern-day Nebraska to Mexico and from modern-day Texas to Arizona. The heart of this territory is the modern American Southwest. This area is a rough land of deserts and mountains.

The Apache people moved widely within their homeland. Some groups had farms where they spent time and grew crops each year. All Apache families traveled throughout the seasons. They went to places where they could find food, water, and good weather. Sometimes they built villages. They stayed in these villages for several months each year. But more often, they built camps in places where conditions were best.

In the eastern Apache homeland, wide plains and prairies make up the landscape. The Kiowa-Apaches hunted the great herds of buffalo that once lived there. Buffalo became their main supply of food. And buffalo skins were an important part of Apache homes.

In this painting, Native Americans are hunting buffalo. Some Apache groups hunted buffalo for food and animal hides.

The Apaches built two kinds of homes. Eastern Apache groups built tipis *(above)*. Tipis were made from wood poles and buffalo hides. They were easy to set up and take down.

The people in the eastern homeland lived in tipis. These cone-shaped homes were made of buffalo hides laid over a frame of wooden poles. An opening in one side served as a door. Inside, a fire burned in the center of the tipi. A hole at the top of the cone let out the smoke.

Fewer buffalo lived in the western homeland. In this region, the Apache people hunted other animals for food. They also lived in different homes, called *gowa*. Sometimes gowa are also called wickiups. Like tipis, these homes were round and built out of poles. Instead of using buffalo hides as covers, Apache people used bear grass or other leaves and brush. A family built new gowa when they moved to a new place.

Whether they lived in tipis or wickiups, Apaches traveled light. Their homes had little furniture. They took with them only the most important tools for gathering food and setting up a camp at their next stop.

This painting from the 1800s shows an Apache husband and wife outside their gowa.

FAMILY LIFE

The Apaches lived very independently. They did not form one main government. Instead, Apache communities were based on families. Apache life revolved around family. When an Apache couple married, the husband came to live with his bride's relatives. Big families often traveled together, including grandparents, aunts, and uncles. Several families might form a small group called a band. A well-respected man usually led the band.

This photograph of an Apache family was taken in the late 1800s. The Apache people often lived in family groups.

An Apache woman takes care of the family cornfield. She is carrying her baby on her back. In many family groups, Apache women or men farmed.

Apache women took care of the home. When a family or band reached a new stopping place, women built the tipis or wickiups. Later, they kept them clean and well organized. Women also had the job of gathering food, such as berries, nuts, and seeds.

Most Apaches also farmed small pieces of land. They raised crops, such as corn, pumpkins, and beans. In some groups, women planted and cared for the fields. In others, men did the farming.

While women took care of the camp and household, Apache men did the hunting. They hunted buffalo and other large animals such as deer. They also hunted smaller creatures, such as rabbits.

When the hunters returned to camp with animals, women prepared the meat for eating. They cut some of it into long strips and dried it in the sun to make jerky. This dried meat could last for many weeks.

A Native American man hunts antelope. Apache men hunted with bows and arrows. They sometimes wore animal skins so they could get close to creatures they hunted.

A Native American woman dries meat. The Apache
dried meat to make jerky and pemmican.

They also made a food called pemmican out of
lean meat. After they had dried the meat, they
pounded it into powder. Then they mixed it with
melted fat. Sometimes Apache cooks added dried
fruit to the pemmican for extra flavor and vitamins.

Apaches used more than just the meat of
animals. Apache women sewed blankets, shirts,
dresses, and shoes from the skins. They used
sinews, or tendons, for thread. Bones and teeth
became parts of tools such as knives. And
stomachs were used as canteens.

A young Apache woman poses with her baskets in the early 1900s. Apache women were very skilled basket makers.

Apache women also used other materials to make household items. Their special skill was making baskets. They wove these out of plant fibers. Baskets were both beautiful and useful. They held food, water, and other items.

Apache girls helped their mothers with all these tasks. They learned the skills that they would need when they became wives and mothers. Meanwhile, boys learned the ways of hunting from their fathers.

Apache children worked alongside their parents. But they also played. Games and fun were part of Apache childhood. Children had a special place in the community. They were well loved and cared for. And they learned important lessons about Apache life.

A WORLD OF SPIRITS

Apache children learned about their people's spiritual beliefs. The Apaches believed that their homeland was filled with spiritual power and meaning. All things, from the moon and the mountains to animals and plants, held that spiritual power.

Apache children pose by their house in the late 1880s. Children are an important part of the Apache community.

Pesh-Coo *(left)* was an Apache shaman. He was a spiritual leader and healer for his people during the late 1800s.

Many spirits lived in the homeland. But some spirits were friendlier than others. Ghosts and witches could bring bad luck. And being respectful to all spirits was important. Making them angry could cause illnesses or other misfortunes.

Shaman men and women led spiritual events called ceremonies. These ceremonies included dancing, singing, and prayer. Sometimes they were used to give thanks for good fortune. Other ceremonies were used to heal sick people. Sometimes shamans used herbs and other plants as medicine.

Over the years, some Apache bands developed different beliefs. But their basic shared ideas helped connect all Apache people.

In this color drawing, a Native American shaman performs a healing ceremony. Apache shamans healed the sick with similar ceremonies. They also created medicines from plants and herbs.

CHAPTER 2

NEIGHBORS AND NEWCOMERS

THE APACHES WERE NOT ALONE IN THE SOUTHWEST. The Pueblos, a large Native American group, also lived there. At first, Apaches and Pueblos lived mostly in peace with one another. Sometimes they traded goods. The Pueblos lived in villages and farmed the land around their homes. They offered the Apaches crops, cloth, pottery, and other items. In return, Apache traders gave the Pueblos meat and skins from wild game.

But Apaches weren't always friendly with other Native Americans. Apaches sometimes took supplies from other groups. They stole animals and food in raids on Pueblo villages. They also raided the camps of other nearby groups.

These raids rarely involved any fighting. They were quick and usually took place at night. But conflicts did sometimes break out between different groups. Apaches could be injured or killed in these fights. When that happened, Apache warriors felt that it was their duty to get back at the enemy.

Two Pueblo men appear in traditional dress in the early 1900s. The Apaches and the Pueblos shared part of a common homeland.

Apache warriors made many of their weapons, including lances and bows and arrows. Europeans introduced guns to the Apaches.

Apache men were in charge of raids and warfare. Weapon making was also a job for the men. They crafted bows and arrows and long spears called lances. Just as Apache boys learned about hunting from their male relatives, they also learned the ways of war.

The Apaches were good warriors. They fought for food, supplies, and survival. And when they felt they had been wronged, they fought for their honor. Over the years, their enemies came to know them as fierce and frightening.

STRANGERS APPEAR

In 1541, life for all Native Americans in the Southwest changed forever. That year, Spanish explorers arrived in the region. They came looking for gold and silver. The Spanish did not find as much treasure as they had hoped. But they did find a new land with many resources.

The Spanish arrived in the Southwest riding powerful horses. Apaches had never seen horses before. But they soon realized how helpful these animals could be.

Spaniard Francisco Coronado and his men arrive in the present-day western United States. Coronado introduced horses to the Southwest.

Apache people ride horses during the early 1900s. Spanish explorers brought the first horses to the Apache homeland.

In hard times, hungry Apaches could kill and eat horses. But Apaches also began using the animals for much more than food. Horses helped them travel faster and farther. Women rode horses to gather foods growing far from camp. Men used them for hunting and raiding. Horses were a good addition to the Apache way of life.

But the Spanish also brought misery and death to the region. As time went on, they set up large ranches and farms in the Southwest. They needed workers for their fields. So they fought the Pueblo people and forced them to work.

The Spanish did not conquer the Apache people. The Apaches were skilled warriors. And they knew the best places in their homeland to hide. These skills helped keep most of them free. But the Spanish did capture some Apaches. They kept or sold these prisoners as slaves, bringing great sorrow to the Apache people.

DANGEROUS MISSIONS

Throughout the Southwest, the Spanish set up forts to protect their territory. They also set up Christian churches called missions. Many missions offered Native Americans food and shelter in return for work. Some Apaches accepted. But the work was hard, and the food was barely enough. Church workers called missionaries also tried to force Apaches and other Indians to become Christians. Most Apaches fought against these changes. Sometimes they attacked the missionaries or burned the churches.

This color drawing is of a Pueblo warrior. Spaniards conquered the Pueblo people during the 1500s. Spanish control of the Pueblo Indians took an important trade partner away from the Apaches.

The defeat of the Pueblos was a problem for the Apaches. The defeated Pueblos could not trade anymore. They still lived in their villages, but they had no freedom. The Spanish controlled them.

But Apaches still needed the supplies the Pueblos had given them. Apache men began raiding village farmers and Spanish settlements. They raided Spanish settlements for horses. In the 1600s, Apache raids continued.

VIOLENT YEARS

In the early 1700s, Comanche Indians began expanding their territory in the Southwest. The

Comanches were strong fighters. Their attacks pushed the eastern Apaches farther south and west.

As Apache territory shrank, so did food sources. Apache warriors made even more raids against other Indians. The Apaches moved even deeper into Spanish territory to the south. Apache raids against the Spanish became more common and more violent. In turn, the Spanish made harsher attacks of their own.

This mural shows Comanche warriors. The Comanches moved into the Apache homeland during the 1700s.

The ruins of a Spanish mission stand in the Arizona desert. Apache raids forced the Spanish and the Pima Indians to leave the mission.

The Spanish and Apaches tried several times to make peace in the 1700s. But real peace was not easy because the Apaches had no single leader. Different bands fought different settlements independently. One band of Apaches might agree to stop raiding, while others kept fighting. The Spanish also raided some peaceable Apaches. So peace never held for very long. The violence and death grew worse on both sides.

For a little while in the early 1800s, it seemed like the battles might end. Mexicans had decided that they wanted to be free from Spanish rule. They fought for their independence. And they won it in 1821. The Spanish left the Southwest. But the Mexicans did not have the strength to fight against the Apaches. Apaches attacked Mexican towns to get food and other supplies. And the terrible cycle of warfare went on.

Mexicans celebrate their independence from Spain in 1821. Mexicans and the Apaches continued to fight over land.

CHAPTER 3

FIRST MEETINGS AND LAST STANDS

IN THE 1820S AND 1830S, ANOTHER GROUP ARRIVED IN THE APACHE HOMELAND. This time, they came from the east.

The United States was then only about fifty years old. It was still small. And most of its land was east of the Apache homeland. But people in the new nation were eager to explore. They had already started moving west.

At first, most Apaches and white Americans were friendly with one another. But the Apaches had been fighting the Spanish and Mexicans for a long time. They were not sure if they could trust these new outsiders. And the white settlers had their own goals. They hoped to make their young country bigger. Settlers and their families joined the push to the West. They came looking for land and wealth.

U.S. settlers move into the West during the 1800s. The Apaches were not sure they could trust their new neighbors.

U.S. soldiers celebrate a victory over the Mexican army during the Mexican-American War (1846–1848). The United States won Apache lands from Mexico after winning the war in 1848.

Then, in 1846, the United States and Mexico went to war. Both countries wanted land in the Southwest. The United States won the Mexican-American War in 1848. The United States took control of much of the Apache homeland. More white settlers than ever streamed into the Southwest. And gold was found in California in 1849. Then even more people arrived. They hoped to strike it rich in the gold mines.

New people meant new hunters. More people meant more homes, which used more wood. But the growth of ranches had the greatest effect. Ranchers needed lots of land for their cows and horses. The animals and plants that Apaches had used for centuries had to be shared by more and more people.

To make matters worse, most Americans thought that Apaches and other Native Americans were not civilized. They thought that whites were better than these people. And they believed that they had more right to the land than American Indians did.

U.S. ranchers needed a lot of space for huge herds of cattle. Ranchers often wanted Apache land.

But Apaches were ready to protect their own way of life. They would keep fighting for their homeland.

WAGING WAR

Problems between whites and the Apaches grew during the mid-1800s. In 1861, they erupted into war. A bloody wave of battles swept the Southwest. Apache leaders such as Mangas Coloradas and Cochise led warriors against the whites. The U.S. Army also sent well-armed troops westward.

An Apache warrior aims at a wagon train. The Apaches began to fight against settlement of their homeland in the mid-1800s.

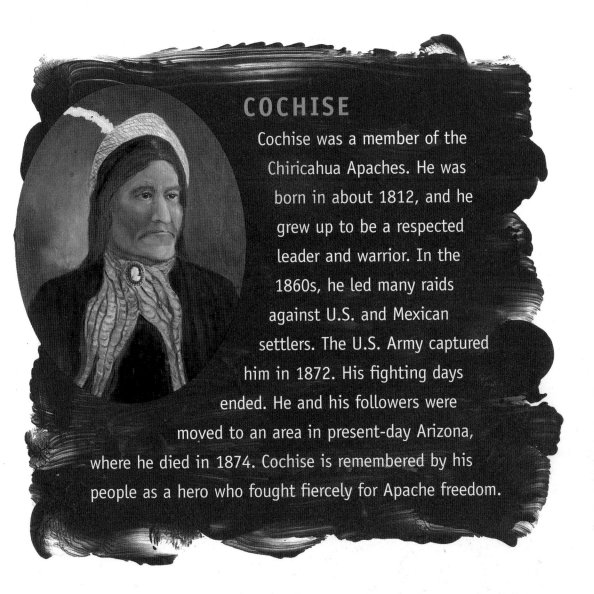

COCHISE

Cochise was a member of the Chiricahua Apaches. He was born in about 1812, and he grew up to be a respected leader and warrior. In the 1860s, he led many raids against U.S. and Mexican settlers. The U.S. Army captured him in 1872. His fighting days ended. He and his followers were moved to an area in present-day Arizona, where he died in 1874. Cochise is remembered by his people as a hero who fought fiercely for Apache freedom.

But white settlers still had trouble defending themselves. Apaches could strike quickly and then disappear into the wilderness. At this time, the United States was also in the middle of the Civil War (1861–1865). This war kept most of the army busy.

Government officials tried other ways of dealing with the Apaches. They offered the Apaches treaties. These agreements promised peace in return for land or goods. But the Americans often broke their promises. Each time a treaty fell apart, the Apaches trusted the United States less.

The U.S. government also created areas called reservations. These plots of land were set aside just for Native Americans. Government officials told the Apaches to stop fighting and move to the

U.S. soldiers fight with Apache warriors. The U.S. government used warfare and treaties to try to control the Apaches.

This painting shows an Apache meeting with a U.S. official. Government leaders promised Apaches land and goods for peace agreements. The government often broke these treaties.

reservations. If the Apaches agreed, the officials promised they could live there in peace.

Peace sounded good to most Apaches. They were tired of fighting a battle that seemed endless and impossible to win. More white settlers seemed to arrive in the Southwest each day. In the end, many Apaches agreed to move onto reservations. They were sad to give up the independence that they had always enjoyed. But they were also afraid for the future of their people.

SAD DAYS

Reservation life turned out to be very hard. The reservations were usually too small for so many people. They were often in uncomfortable and unhealthy places. There was not enough food or housing. And the officials who ran the reservations were sometimes unkind or unfair.

The Apache people were used to roaming freely. They hated the new way of life. Some escaped

An Apache mother and her daughter cook a meal on a reservation. Life on the reservations could be hard.

May Apaches refused to live on reservations.
These Apaches often fought for their freedom.

from the reservations. They often went back to
raiding. Some of these attacks were for survival.
Others were to get back at their enemies.

Cochise continued to fight against white
settlers. But he surrendered in 1872. A warrior
named Victorio and his followers kept up the
struggle. They fought against both Americans and
Mexicans until 1880.

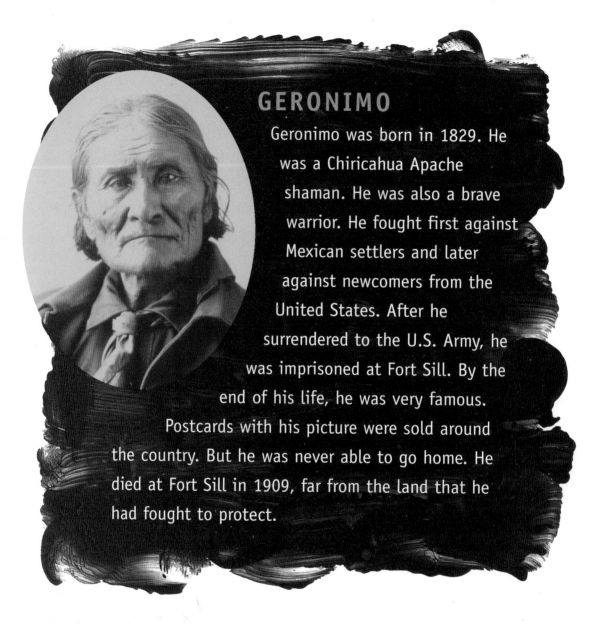

GERONIMO

Geronimo was born in 1829. He was a Chiricahua Apache shaman. He was also a brave warrior. He fought first against Mexican settlers and later against newcomers from the United States. After he surrendered to the U.S. Army, he was imprisoned at Fort Sill. By the end of his life, he was very famous. Postcards with his picture were sold around the country. But he was never able to go home. He died at Fort Sill in 1909, far from the land that he had fought to protect.

Finally, only one major Apache warrior remained free. Geronimo and a band of fighters still held out against white soldiers. But Geronimo was forced to surrender in 1886. He and hundreds of other Apache prisoners were loaded into trains. They were sent across the country to a prison in Florida. Later, they were moved to a fort in Alabama and finally to Fort Sill in Oklahoma.

The Apache prisoners were put in cramped, dirty camps. Many died. The survivors became known as the Fort Sill Apaches. They were never allowed to go back to their homelands.

Geronimo's defeat was the end of an era. He and his band had been the last Apaches to resist white control.

Geronimo *(center)* and his fighters gather for battle. Geronimo surrendered to the U.S. government in 1886.

CHAPTER 4

NEW BEGINNINGS

COCHISE, GERONIMO, AND OTHER FIGHTERS HAD FOUGHT AGAINST CHANGES TO THEIR WAY OF LIFE. But for Apaches living on reservations, life had already changed greatly.

Reservations limited the Apaches' freedom. Like the Spanish, many Americans tried to convert Apaches to Christianity. They also taught them English. They tried to change Apache styles of dress and housing. Adults were told to do jobs that did not fit in with their usual family roles. All these events changed the Apache way of life.

Many children were taken and sent to schools in other parts of the United States. For close-knit Apache families, being separated was painful. And Apache students at boarding schools no longer learned traditional ways from their parents. Sometimes their Apache names were even changed to ones that sounded more European American.

In the late 1800s, many Native Americans were sent to Indian boarding schools. The U.S. government used these schools to make Native American children learn white American ways.

A VOICE OF THEIR OWN

Apaches were angry about all these changes. They spoke up for their rights. Other people also looked for ways to improve life for American Indians. In the 1930s, new laws gave Apaches more control over the reservations. Many Apache groups began organizing their own governments.

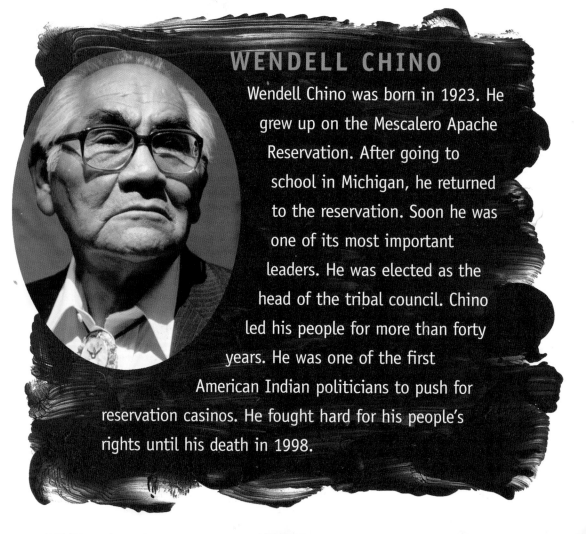

WENDELL CHINO

Wendell Chino was born in 1923. He grew up on the Mescalero Apache Reservation. After going to school in Michigan, he returned to the reservation. Soon he was one of its most important leaders. He was elected as the head of the tribal council. Chino led his people for more than forty years. He was one of the first American Indian politicians to push for reservation casinos. He fought hard for his people's rights until his death in 1998.

A Native American man protests the treatment of American Indians in the 1970s. Apaches and other Native Americans began to organize for their rights in the 1960s.

In the 1960s and 1970s, Native Americans all over the country continued to speak out for their rights. Apaches and other American Indians gained more and more independence.

Just like in the past, no single organization speaks for all the Apache people. But separate groups have their own tribal governments. Apaches vote for leaders to guide their communities. They have a say in their people's lives and their future.

In the 1980s, there were only a few businesses on Apache reservations. Apaches and their leaders thought of ways to bring jobs and money to their reservations.

BIG BUSINESS

In the 1980s, the Apaches were a strong people. They had won many rights. But they still faced challenges. Most Apaches on reservations had little money and few job opportunities. Some leaders began talking about new ways to earn money. One idea was to open casinos on the reservations.

Casinos are places where adults can play games for money. Playing these games is called gambling.

Most U.S. states have laws against this type of gambling. But a new law in 1988 said that reservation governments did not have to follow all state laws. They were independent.

The first Apache casinos were a big success. One of the biggest was on the Mescalero Apache Reservation in New Mexico. It still attracts visitors from New Mexico and beyond.

This casino is on the Mescalero reservation. Casinos have been successful businesses for some Apache groups.

Apache businesspeople opened hotels and restaurants for the visitors. These new businesses made new jobs. Many Mescalero Apaches were able to earn more money and live better lives.

MODERN LIFE

In the 2000s, more than fifty thousand Apaches live in the United States. About forty thousand more Americans are part Apache. Modern Apaches

CELEBRATING THE SUNRISE

Modern Apaches still celebrate long-honored spiritual traditions. One important celebration is the Sunrise Dance. This event celebrates an Apache girl's change from a child into a woman. The dance lasts several days. Teenage girls wear special clothes and take part in singing, dancing, and prayer. Through these rituals, the girls connect with White-Painted Woman. This powerful female spirit is very important to Apache beliefs. Families and friends gather to be part of this moment in an Apache girl's life.

These Apaches are firefighters. Apache people hold many kinds of jobs on reservations and across the United States.

live all across the United States. They hold many different jobs and lead all kinds of lifestyles.

More than twenty thousand Apaches live on reservations. Most Apache reservations are in the Southwest. The largest is the San Carlos Reservation near Phoenix, Arizona. Other major reservations include Arizona's White Mountain Apache Reservation and New Mexico's Mescalero Apache Reservation and Jicarilla Apache Nation.

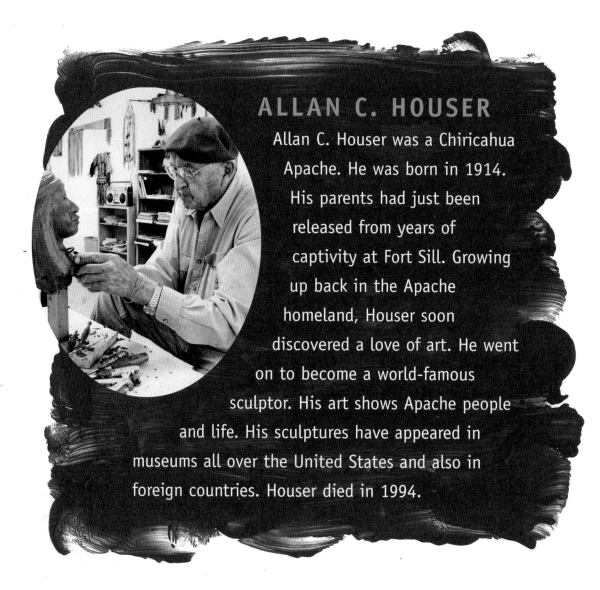

ALLAN C. HOUSER

Allan C. Houser was a Chiricahua Apache. He was born in 1914. His parents had just been released from years of captivity at Fort Sill. Growing up back in the Apache homeland, Houser soon discovered a love of art. He went on to become a world-famous sculptor. His art shows Apache people and life. His sculptures have appeared in museums all over the United States and also in foreign countries. Houser died in 1994.

Life on reservations can still be tough. Some Apaches have successful businesses, such as cattle ranches or lumber companies. Others hold valuable natural resources, such as oil and natural gas. And tourism is big business for some reservations. The beautiful Apache homeland draws many travelers each year. Reservations with casinos, golf courses, ski resorts, and other attractions pull in even more visitors. But other reservations' economies are struggling. Many Apaches have trouble finding jobs.

Some Apaches work in traditional jobs. For example, Apache artists still craft beautiful baskets. This work has been part of Apache life for many years.

A modern Apache woman weaves a cradle. Weaving is traditional Apache work.

Apaches celebrate their heritage in other ways too. Dances still honor Apache spiritual beliefs. Community events called powwows bring Apaches and other Native Americans together. Powwows celebrate American Indian culture and beliefs.

Newer traditions are also important to modern Apache life. Rodeos draw large crowds to the reservations. Basketball is a popular sport with many Apache youth.

The Apache people have a past filled with pride and also pain. They treasure their heritage and their traditions. And they look ahead to the future with hope.

Riders compete in a roping contest during an Apache rodeo.

PINE NUT BREAD

2 cups pine nuts (without shells)
¾ cup water
½ teaspoon salt
2 tablespoons lard or vegetable oil

1. Chop pine nuts in a blender or food processor until they are chopped into small pieces. (You can also mash the nuts very well in a mortar and pestle.)
2. In a medium mixing bowl, combine nuts, water, and salt. Mix well. Place the pine nut mixture on a lightly floured countertop or other clean work surface. Knead it by pressing on it with your hands, folding it over, and pressing again. Knead until the mixture is fairly stiff. Set aside at room temperature for about 1 hour.
3. Place lard or oil in a large skillet. Heat over medium heat until a drop of water sizzles on the skillet's surface.
4. Carefully drop about one tablespoonful of batter into the skillet. Using a spatula, flatten the ball of batter into a patty. Repeat with remaining batter.
5. Reduce heat slightly and cook each patty for about 2 to 3 minutes on each side, or until golden brown. Remove from heat, and serve bread hot or cold.

Makes about 12 patties

PLACES TO VISIT

Fort Apache Historic Park
Fort Apache, Arizona
(928) 338-1230
http://www.wmat.nsn.us/fortapachepark.htm
This park is on Arizona's White Mountain Apache Reservation. It
includes the old fort plus a cultural center and museum.

Fort Sill National Historic Landmark
Fort Sill, Oklahoma
(580) 442-5123
http://sill-www.army.mil/Museum/
This historic fort is where Geronimo and other Apache captives were
held between 1886 and 1914. The site includes a museum.

Jicarilla Apache Nation
Dulce, New Mexico
(505) 759-3242
http://jicarillaonline.com/
Visitors to the Jicarilla Apache Nation's reservation in northern New
Mexico can enjoy events such as the annual Go-Jii-Yah Feast. This
September celebration includes activities such as rodeos, footraces,
and a powwow.

National Museum of the American Indian
Washington, D.C.
(202) 633-1000
http://www.nmai.si.edu/
This museum is part of the Smithsonian Institution. It features
exhibits about the history and culture of Apaches as well as other
Native American groups.

GLOSSARY

band: a group of several Apache clans

clan: a group of several Apache families who lived and traveled together

gowa: a dome-shaped home made of poles covered with straw, grasses, and other plants. Apaches lived in gowa, also called wickiups, in the Southwest.

missionaries: people who try to persuade others to adopt their religion

Native Americans: people who have lived in North or South America for hundreds of years

pemmican: a food made from dried and powdered meat mixed with melted fat and sometimes dried berries or other fruit

raid: a quick attack on a camp or settlement, usually to get food and other supplies

reservations: areas of land set aside by the U.S. government for use by particular American Indian groups

shamans: Apache spiritual leaders. Shamans could be male or female and were sometimes called medicine men or medicine women.

tipis: cone-shaped homes made of wooden poles covered with buffalo skins. Many Apaches in the eastern homeland lived in tipis.

treaty: a written agreement between two or more nations or groups

FURTHER READING

Early, Theresa S. *New Mexico*. Minneapolis: Lerner Publications Company, 2003. Discover more about New Mexico, one of the central states in the Apache homeland.

Filbin, Dan. *Arizona*. Minneapolis: Lerner Publications Company, 2002. Learn about Arizona, home to thousands of Apache people.

Kavasch, E. Barrie. *Apache Children and Elders Talk Together*. New York: PowerKids Press, 1999. Grandchildren and great-grandchildren of Geronimo talk about their family's history and the Apache people.

Lacapa, Michael. *The Flute Player: An Apache Folktale*. Flagstaff, AZ: Northland Publishing, 1990. This picture book retells an Apache story about a young flute player. The tale says that the sound of wind in the Southwest is the sound of his flute.

Phillips, Larissa. *Cochise: Apache Chief*. New York: Rosen Publishing Group, 2004. Learn more about Cochise, a brave Apache leader and warrior.

Welch, Catherine A. *Geronimo*. Minneapolis: Lerner Publications Company, 2004. Explore the life of Geronimo and his fight for freedom.

WEBSITES

Allan Houser: Experience the Work of a Lifetime
http://www.allanhouser.com/
View the official website of Apache artist Allan Houser. Click on the Featured Inventory link to see some of his sculptures.

Apache Language Speaking Dictionary
http://www.wusd.k12.az.us/Links/Staff/BGood/Apachedictionary/
Apachedict.html
Visit this website to hear Apache words and phrases. These sound clips were recorded by Apache high school students from Arizona's White Mountain Apache Reservation.

The Sunrise Dance
  http://www.peabody.harvard.edu/maria/Sunrisedance.html
  Read a detailed description of this important Apache ceremony, from
  Harvard University's Peabody Museum.

SELECTED BIBLIOGRAPHY

Aleshire, Peter. *Reaping the Whirlwind: The Apache Wars*. New York: Facts
  on File, 1998.

Griffin-Pierce, Trudy. *Native Peoples of the Southwest*. Albuquerque:
  University of New Mexico Press, 2000.

Opler, Morris Edward. *An Apache Life-Way: The Economic, Social, and
  Religious Institutions of the Chiricahua Indians*. Lincoln: University of
  Nebraska Press, 1996.

Robinson, Sherry. *Apache Voices: Their Stories of Survival as Told to Eve
  Ball*. Albuquerque: University of New Mexico Press, 2000.

Schweinfurth, Kay Parker. *Prayer on Top of the Earth: The Spiritual
  Universe of the Plains Apaches*. Boulder: University Press of Colorado,
  2002.

Terrell, John Upton. *Apache Chronicle: The Story of the People*. New York:
  Thomas Y. Crowell Company, 1974.

Waldman, Carl. *Encyclopedia of Native American Tribes*. New York: Facts
  on File, 1988.

Watt, Eva Tulene. *Don't Let the Sun Step Over You: A White Mountain
  Apache Family Life*. Tucson: University of Arizona Press, 2004.

INDEX